GLOBE

MICHEAL O'SIADHAIL

GLOBE

BLOODAXE BOOKS

ISBN: 978 1 85224 757 7

First published 2007 by
Bloodaxe Books Ltd,
Highgreen,
Tarset,
Northumberland NE48 1RP.

www.bloodaxebooks.com
For further information about Bloodaxe titles
please visit our website or write to
the above address for a catalogue.

Bloodaxe Books Ltd acknowledges
the financial assistance of
Arts Council England, North East.

Cover design: Neil Astley & Pamela Robertson-Pearce.

Cover printing: J. Thomson Colour Printers Ltd, Glasgow.

Printed in Great Britain by
Bell & Bain Limited, Glasgow, Scotland.

For David, friend of friends

Our dance within the isotope
Ties and tears of history's robe;
Born in a land, I wake in a globe.

ACKNOWLEDGEMENTS

Acknowledgements are due to the editors of the following publications, in which some of these poems first appeared: *An Easter People: Essays in Honour of Sr Stanislaus Kennedy* (Veritas, 2005), *David Jones Society Journal*, *Other Poetry*, *The Stinging Fly* and *Tsunami* (Trinity College Dublin Press, 2005).

CONTENTS

ANGEL OF CHANGE

SHADOW-MARKS

...while memory holds a seat
in this distracted globe.

WILLIAM SHAKESPEARE

Given

Duke Ellington's It don't mean a thing
(If it ain't got that swing) juggles a gene
From within a phrase. Newness takes wing.

Our human being one second in three years;
As an atom to the planet our earth in space,
A single offbeat in all that jazz of spheres.

Still somehow the player's nerve to chance it,
Even to love a humbler in-betweenness
Of non-stop becoming, to flourish in transit.

O world as it is and not as it might have been,
Our riven map of this cussed here and now
Where webs and clusters of movers again begin

To allow the to and fro of things to arrange
And rearrange while another bridge passage
Prepares tomorrow's loops and modes of change.

For all our line's fragilities still dream-driven
As shifting landscapes shape and are reshaped.
Our one precious second. Our globe as given.

Shift

All generations face up to this
Slippage of what's familiar, slidings,
Differences of use and tone,
Subtle plays of emphasis,
Things
That steal up on us and push us on.

The way a word's meaning shifts
And though some resist or gripe
Most don't notice any move
As one strong verb shifts
Type
To settle down in another groove

Which bit by bit starts a pattern
That just may or may not take
But even if it does that too
Will of course in its turn
Break,
Making way for something new

So we slowly accumulate a past
In stirring of grammar's overspill
Which seems to allow us both
A sense of what's steadfast
And still
To feel the sway and pull of growth

Unless some sudden unforeseen
Upheaval or leap brings so swift
A change our whole context
Alters, a switch of scene,
A rift
Between one era and the next.

Under our noses this giddy pace.
Backfooted, an old paradigm
Unravels and all's at stake
As we melodeon space
And time.
Globe unmapped, globe we make.

Mobile

Once our globe of heartache, a long ago
Of emigrant wake and no return but now

Across all busy skies the prodded phone.
Nihau! thumbs a sojourner in China Town.

Each node of belonging homed by satellite
Travels the dark fibres of a breakfast update

To touch digital nerves of daily memory.
'O you're my life that began...' *Inta umri* –

An Arab's Hamburg cab plays Umm Kulthum.
On worldwide webs our charted genome,

Eons of software copied from pod to pod,
A narrative mapped in one meandering code.

Lenses of time and space now telescope
And the long reels of a plot are speeding up

As lineaments of so many histories cross
A blurred zigzag between a "them" and "us".

Our line of country shifts and reconfigures.
We are the world. The face of the earth is ours.

Sputnik

Was it make believe of childhood
That made the garden chosen seem
A time when our lives stayed still

Before the half-remembered thrill
At how a Russian sputnik hurtled
Ring a ring a rosie around an earth.

We didn't know they put a girth
On a patchwork fractious planet.
Tischa, Tischa, walls fall down.

A world that was a collective noun
Snapped from there outside itself,
A whirling clod once photographed

For good a delicate spinning craft,
Pocketful of posies we relearn
To tend, this fragile raft in space.

Everywhere becomes everyplace.
No man is an island Donne knew
Before the instant image wheel

Relayed the tube's mute appeal.
Hungry or broken, the wallfallen
Commands seen in Abel's face.

Tsunami

津
波

1

An unheard inner molten command
And the earth's maw begins to retch
Cracking the floor of the Indian Ocean.

Tsu: water and a brush in hand
To sign a sweep of sea, a stretch
Of deep for safe crossing, a haven.

Nami: liquid and a flaying hand
To symbolise a wave, as if to sketch
An ocean peeling off its skin.

Together a billowing towards land,
A tidal wave gathering its fetch
To deliver a long roll of misfortune.

2

Their flight visceral
And inborn as before it begins
An original
People still read the signs.

Nature's bonds
Broken by stilted inn
Or shrimp ponds
No mangroves hold the line.

Safer at sea:
In shallows the swells heighten,
Irony
Of a harbour now danger's haven.

Earthlings our toss
And turn frail in the sweep
Of a cosmos,
Humble riders on a moody spaceship,

A trembling globe.
Some hundred and eighty thousand.
Like Job
We cry out what is our end?

3

That all would have died sometime.
Any death as much a riddle as thousands.
So many together, unripe, in their prime?

Whole kindred with no one to claim
Their hurried dead or still to remember
A vanished face or a cried name.

Never to be called 'old man' *Bapak!*
Days into days stretch into weeks
And tides sweep over the crack

As an orphan blows her toy trumpet
Sumatra's grievers show signs of return
Setting out fruits at a morning market.

Durian, papaya, lime and mangostan.
Our earth is spinning across its seasons.
Fishermen cling to the skin of an ocean.

Underground

Scoops once cabled along an ocean's bed
Bounce their waves in space as each report
Lets us for a while turn brothers' keepers.

But news is news and another item dead.
A sense of stretching, always falling short;
Prisoners of each instant, global peepers.

Turnover. Overload. Through-put. Burn-out.
Simultaneous broadcast, performance of now,
Take it or leave it, our all-consuming present.

Choices. Options. Preferences. All about
Freedom to zap and channel-hop, to allow
Us our daily shop around in any event.

Cameramen fly on to break another story
Across a dimming or warming atmosphere,
A jet-stream of bulletins for fear we'd wake

To stale headlines. Our yesterday is history.
Through windows of planes beginning to near
A runway reporters stare down as though to take

A reading of another landscape's hints and signs
On patches of an archaeologist's aerial photo
Spreading under their vapour trailing air-bus

Shadow-marks the rape's yellow outlines
Over sites of older settlements bedded below.
Underground shine of bones foreshadow us.

Touch-down

In all our moods and changes some groundplot,
Some sense of what was to give us bearings,
A recorder tuning in to where we were;
Even in such doubting days when we're aware
How grand flight plans so often clip the wings
Of underlings to justify the have and have-not.

Cold comfort in the cosy no-man's-land
Of huffing theorists busy trying to climb
Out of history, seeing everywhere deceits,
The half-aware cheatings of previous elites
Or reaching back to chide another time
Where long ago is a city built on sand

Of disillusion at ideas so fallen from grace
Once they knew explained the line and sweep
Of certain progress, stage by stage ascent
Of man and so their fingers burnt they're bent
On undermining everything, determined to keep
Cutting off our nose to spite our face.

Hail! all smothered voices from the past,
Orphan written out, forgotten dissenter
And every saga left too long untold,
Come in now waif and nomad from the cold!
The margins edge out a blurring centre,
Let the broken come into their own at last.

Still in curves and echoes of polyphony gone
Before us, a tune that's both old and fresh
Among the ties and leaps of complex histories
Allows the resonance and unforeseen of stories'
Shifts and vamped progressions that seem to mesh
Plots wound deep in us and winding on

Into the blue of other flights and offbeat
Loop the loops to retrieve out of the lurch
Of fashion things we thought we'd outgrown,
Out of date jingles on a mobile telephone

Where we just scroll quickly down to search
Our main menu's options and thumb *delete*.

Deafness of now in each newsflash and cast
As if too present we only hear the status
Quo of notes, missing out the arch of sound
Soaring its riffs above some older ground
Base phrase where our ghosts still nod at us.
This touching down in the lift-off of our past.

Scenario

In a rim's touch and turn
Our moment's wheel of now
Already become what was.

All that's to come still jazz,
An unknown latent in know-how;
Our past a future we learn.

Perspective

1 *Middle Distance*

We learn the touch-and-go of being
Between, figures in a half-distance,
Neither a loom too close to view
Or a shape so vague as not to matter
Rather brokers in the thick of things,
Movers in a loose focus of betwixtness
We walk a canvas's middle ground.

2 *Wide Angle*

So deep our mind's desire for seeing
Grander sweeps, a craving to glance
An overall or in detachment to eschew
Events that seem no more than a spatter
Of foam on the tides history brings
To swirl our lives along regardless,
Broadbrush of aeons in the round,

Great vistas and trends decreeing
Our civilisations' first appearance –
Booms and slumps, how they grew,
Why they flourish, then shatter,
Rise and fall determined by curvings
Of coast or river, Nile or Euphrates
The land-locked or the outward bound.

Does what at first may seem a freeing
Turn us all to slaves of circumstance?
Our long slow story lines accrue
Clusters of growth in the teeming clatter
And confusion of so many happenings,
Thousands of encounters in our daily mess,
In the bigger picture's blurred surround.

3 *Close-up*

And some scale downward, fleeing
The muddle in labyrinths of remembrance,
In scents and musks of Proust's clew
Winding inward a psyche's chatter
With warts and all foreshortenings,
Chosen myopia of endless consciousness,
An insomniac's inner merry-go-round,

Recalls of detail that though guaranteeing
Darker oubliettes of self still unbalance
What we think and what we do.
A worn-in narrative is both flatter
And richer for our shared humdrummings
Where inner and outer worlds caress,
The commonplaces that still astound.

4 *Symmetry*

Even our own heart-beat is keying
Us to the middle of a cosmic dance;
Our pulse a geometric average of two
Limits: from the Big Bang's scatter
It's fifteen billion years, the swing
Of atoms a femto-world. O Antaeus
Keep your airy feet on the ground.

Footprint

Sometimes ground vanishes under our feet
As tidal waves of change sweep in so fast
Over sand too shifting now for any retreat.

But neither fogeys nor spirit-rappers of a past,
All thumbs, slowly we text our mobile tidings
Copping on to Gr8 & c u @ 3.

The only rule of thumb to learn new things
As our middle voice tips towards passivity
Allowing another generation show us how

To program memories and delete what's old
Or out-of-date as making way we bow
With grace to let another crowd take hold.

Even in the thrill and confusion of letting go
Strange continuities in this thumb tick-tack
A sign from school or invoices (*so and so*

Many @ such and such) makes a come-back.
Yet also some unease lurks in the marrow
That those who follow us may thumb their nose

At footprints we'd walked in, once numinous
Traces rubbed out by history's ebbs and flows
In the sifting sand-glass of our remembrance.

Under their thumbs one global city they build;
Their turn to find loops and detours of advance,
Keeping promises we're leaving unfulfilled.

Thread Mark

Who'll promise to remember us?
An angel of change has brushed its wing
against the frail contours of our lives.

A lighter generation now takes off.
Open-ended travellers. Will they become
globe-trotters, strays and passers-by,

our turn a past they won't recall
as their own? Already a future forebears
once imagined now long outdated.

O angel of history must we forget
those hard-earned vestiges in our clay,
sweat of heritage, arrears we owe?

The dues paid, the debt assumed,
our thread mark of owing between
those who were and those who follow.

Yes, to love the flow, to embrace
the shifting globe and yet the risk
of traces lost in giddiness of change.

In these fragmented times we wonder
will those who fit the prints we leave
remember feet that walked before them?

Slope

So frail the ways that we remember,
Episodes we fudge or blur,
The unconscious ember
We keep on raking over

And just ordinary hit and miss
Of human recall, hazed
In some failed synapsis,
A sign in our psyche's wax erased

Or even the way our status quo
Chooses a founding memory
It was always so,
How we were and how we'll be.

One narrative, an ancient nation,
Flag and parade and anthem,
Tyrannies of commemoration
Of us always different from them.

In our stumblings, even in our flaws
And gaps what else have we
But spoors in the mind, our gauze
Of story grown in a womb of memory,

Testimonies of what happened then
Probed and sifted through,
Unfolded and told again,
Our slope of past climbed anew

To fight against the grinding dust
Of forgetfulness and snatch
The absent back? We trust
Now traces of our gone to catch

Between rungs of time's vertigo
Memories of things done
And hallow the dead we owe.
For all our frailty, a risk we run.

Sifting

In all these leap years of change
How easily from heights of now
We view what was as obsolete
Forgetting how
So many things loop and repeat
As gain and loss rearrange,

How in this upping of our pace
What's knitted over centuries
Could unravel half-unnoticed.
Behind our ease
A velvet glove and greedy fist,
Soft tyranny of the market-place,

Bytes of facts and hardnosed
Figures, our problems best
Scanned by instruments. Screening
Out the rest,
We quickly lose a thread of memory,
The poetry in us so readily prosed.

Given a globe of sudden upheaval,
We thrill at change but fear chaos.
In dizzy worlds that begin
To criss-cross
And fuse, we can only trust in
Loops and circuits of retrieval

As trade winds shift and sweep
Over older boundaries
And faithful to our past's debt
We sift memories
For what to recall, what to forget
To steady us now before we leap.

Tension

Any variation a leap in the dark:
Forgetting too little or not remembering enough
We'd stray too long off the beat.

For fear that we might lose the spark
Of what's always more we dare or bluff
Nervy completeness of the incomplete,

Sweet tensions of not yet and memory
Between anticipation and fond repeat,
Interplay of riff and debt.

All our jazzing still an extempore
Of players who know freedom's bittersweet
In every newness they beget.

Brokerage

How begot, how nourished? Reply, reply.
Bred both in the heart and head
and nurtured in the middle ground
of our belongings,

friends, lovers, fellow-players,
darings of trust, clusters of conversation
bedrock and seedbed, chosen garden
of our becoming.

Born and died on such a date
before we knew or cut short,
a fact of dust in public records
unless some

delight in our coming, meaning-makers
who, growing into shared memory,
mourn crimson moments of our end.
City within city,

Groundings of our kept promises
feeding whatever newness we attain,
brokering bonds and ties between
each and all.

Blend

Beyond each heartland over millennia
exodus, migration, scattering,
eternal Jew, Chinese sojourner
or wherever green is worn.

Remember how many thrived in Babylon,
exile and rover making good
or darker musics of belonging
blues, calypso, reggae.

As both before Europe's lines and maps
and in gaps and interstices then,
even more so now that all
our frontiers shift and leak.

Every homeland falls short of our desire.
...che retro la memoria non piò ire –
memory can't backtrack –
Dante dreams onward.

Uprootedness, estrangement, our starting again.
As in the beginning and maybe always
blends of memory, story, myth
cross oceans of longing.

Traces

1

An ocean only ever the sum of its drops,
All that we can, even though we know
That of course, another generation chops
And changes, going wherever currents go.
But what traces will any of us now leave?
A comber's tiny eddy that froths and scums
As much as any of our lifetimes will achieve,
A fret in restless floods of what becomes.
No telling the way each sea-change behaves;
A ripple somewhere in the flux and motion,
In the rips and overfalls of loss and gain
Our pebble skims the water, a wave train
Overwhelmed by the flow, swept to an ocean
On ebbtides of stories that once made waves.

2

Still there are a few marked out for greatness.
Remember debates: *history maketh the man*
Or the other way around so some innateness
Chooses doers and heroes catch as catch can.
Surely both a meaning someone wagers on,
A lifelong preparation but also no doubt
The way it happens, this or that liaison,
The fall and ravel of how it all plays out,
Every complex motive we sift and sieve,
The strands given, lines we splice or tie,
Node-workers, knot-tiers, hitch-makers
Slowly we become our own movers and shakers
As plot and characters merge in reasons why,
Our histories still the tangle of lives we live.

3

Some looping in the least expected strand
Too early out may find they've tied a knot
For a world still not ripe to understand
And seem to stand outside the bigger plot.
The lucky may even get their timing right,
Knotting a moment's perfect knot and yet

Others, years ignored, may walk the light
Long enough to see their mend in the net.
Las Casas upsetting everyone's apple-cart
Or Galileo staring out beyond our ken,
Mendel's pea garden's state of the art
Like Meister Bach lost and found again.
A hitch too soon, on time or in hindsight,
The fingered loop or twist its own delight.

4

Over and over again a hasty dream that strives
To short-cut every shaky setback or hiccough,
All the ordinary fumblings of our frail lives,
Desires to broom the world from the ground up.
When too hurried visions have failed or faltered,
The pendulum swung again by those who frown
On any change, the opting out of nothing altered,
Everything imagined as it was handed down.
Bottom up or top down the same particulars,
Shifting minutiae of a slow working through,
In every doing something still left to be done,
Daily revision of broken histories rebegun.
Our knots must hold as easily as they undo;
And still we bless the memory of our stars.

5

For most nothing momentous or too high-flown,
Just some trace laid down, our mark made
In the give and take of lives, a loan of a loan
Passed on as mention of our names will fade.
It's mainly fallen angels with our clayed feet
And yet moments in stories no one has told,
Split seconds of our double time, a pleat
In a cloth of histories that takes so long to unfold.
A promise kept, something done for someone
As rumours of decency gone to ground for years
Re-emerge, the way suddenly in a niece's son
A gene that ducked and weaved then reappears;
Gestures of love on streets of a fragile city,
Memory inscribed in action, a scratch on eternity.

KNOT-TYING

The knotte, that why every tale is toold...

GEOFFREY CHAUCER

Fame

(for Johann Mendel, Bruder Gregor, botanist;
born 22 July 1822, died 6 January 1884)

Bend low in your garden, *Bruder Gregor*,
count and wait, count hybrids you resow
for eight years, thirty thousand plants
you choose to mate by axils, stems, seeds,
shapes and hues, the dwarf and tall you cross,
Watch how a pair of characters refuse to mix
but keeping one, will spare a hidden other
to flare anew across a later generation,
a lost grandparent again breeds through.
Kiss the ground, Gregor, fondle seeds
wrinkled or round, green and yellow pods,
calculate by night the odds for seven traits
to mutate another shuffled year of peas.
Bend, Brother, seize the wonder you unearth,
these throw-backs that neither blend nor thin,
Darwin knew he should but couldn't see,
switches and engines of our mongrelhood.
Now tell great and good how genes play
a mulish hide and seek. Misunderstood
friar snared in a foolish blindman's-buff,
go tell to your heart's desire your sidelined
wonder but is it we who are blindfold, don't
see how we chase and never can catch on?
Despatch reports to Herr Professors *Hinz*
und Kunz. That tiresome friar who somewhere
in his counting garden hunts strange equations
to answer questions that haven't yet been asked.
No basked in glory, Brother. A feverish talk
or two no one notices, a recessive hidden
in a Brno society's journal shelving dust.
So now become Abbot Gregor and wrangle
out your days in a tax row to die
unknown begetter of genes, a wax-winged
Icarus who'd never flown. Young Johann
Mendel, farmer's son, can we call you Hansel
and tell a boy dreaming in a kitchen garden

before a falling tree will maim his father,
before a nervous student flunks exams,
turns Augustinian *Bruder Gregor* by default
or Herr Professor Nägeli can ignore his find,
tell you how a generation after Jánaček's
organ music at your cortège and clearing decks
confrères burn your papers three unknowing
heirs in different parts laboriously repeat
something of the same experiments only undust
your name from library shelves? Mendel's Law.
Fame, Brother Gregor, a fragile gene
Another forty years beyond your garden.

Après Vous Monsieur!

(for Emmanuel Levinas, philosopher;
born 12 January 1906, died Christmas Day 1995)

A father's arms stretch out across a century
to touch five years from either end,
embrace weighted with presentment and memory
fathoming how to mend.
No 'because', just infinite command,
a face hiding more than it will show
calls you hostage and brother's keeper,
keeper even of your keeping me.
Child of Kovno,
Eighty years riding out the trends,
offstage whisper, side-show
to Sartre, de Beauvoir, Derrida and friends,
unrelenting shadow.
Scene shift and it seems as though
lines, byplays, subplots all combined
to cue a late entrance as a slow
voice of asides and rumours wends
into the mind.
Silent weeper of dead barely named,
parents and brothers still behind
each word, each claim counter-claimed,
mined, then undermined,
fearing we might comprehend
a face we daren't even think we know.
One thing said and unsaid over again,
riff and midrash on the same unashamed
and urgent *ditto*:
I'm here, I'm here for you, *hineni!*
No I and Thou or *quid pro quo*,
Seo anseo mé, me voici!
less equal than below
après vous, monsieur, we bow
between a world at Heidegger's clay feet
and long hidden Talmud years
under doyen M. Chouchani
merciless exegete,

between the realms of Abraham and Ulysses,
between a tent-dweller's incomplete
dream who always turns his gaze
to promised lands and the feat
of a homing voyager who may forget
his cunning journey, between the double helix
of heritage, good gene and true,
between Rabbi and Plato always
Jews and Greeks.
Eighty and his rumour flares and spreads apace.
Autrui, the other's face that seeks
me out, a presence already a trace
of what's concealed but speaks:
I am the one thou shalt not kill!
Traveller, traveller, where have you been?
Après vous Monsieur, Madame!
An outsider turns his insistent face.
Stranger, come in.

Lodestar

(for Patrick Kavanagh, poet;
born 21/22 October 1904, died 30 November 1967)

A star rides watery hills of evening gloom:
'Someday they'll say,' he'd insist,
'you dug this ground with me' – Lennon
his friend will recall. Then, answer
yes, outside the whitethorn hedges of Ballyrush
and Gortin after the narrow tyrant's climb
no dreamer realises.

Some misfit gene long before the womb,
an awkward customer at best,
in school-books finds the leaven
for whatever codon or mystic enhancer
feeds the lone psyche's shock and rush
in clumps of nettles and glistening slime
love immortalises.

Never to allow the fame of rustic heirloom,
a Monaghan colourist;
that digger, Tarry Lennon
you remember, no local romancer,
what's true for Drumnagrella is true for Bangladesh,
for this alone the stairs of broken rhyme.
No compromises

but to face a world of failure and yet resume
as above the tired *Weltgeist*
laughter-smothered courage again
begins to praise, cussed freelancer
tilting at grinding mills of angst and anguish;
another day a prophetic enzyme
still improvises

and Kitty Stobling's new outrageous bridegroom,
a wooer too possessed
to scoff at all the tedious men,
to tend to every dog and chancer
who couldn't see in any December whin bush
a wise king. So what the pantomime
of unwon prizes,

let the final Baggot Street sonnets bloom
when after much trouble blest
by canal water, born again
Zenlover whose post-cancer
no caring jag now surrenders afresh,
Meister Eckhart green and sublime.
O God of surprises!

Kafka's mad, Picasso's sad in despair's confining room,
a kamikaze careerist
batters out the sanity of men.
Eden-haunted angel-glancer,
What word in this cantankerous gene made flesh?
Behind, before, beyond its time
A star still rises.

Cue

(for William Shakespeare, playwright and poet;
born 23 (?) April 1564, died 23 April 1616)

What cheer great and most elusive ghost?
All hail good master, so long engraved in us,
we both speak your mind and do not know
what story shaped an extravagant unerring spirit,
a tyger's heart wrapt in a player's hide
who tells everything and nothing, mummer
entering and exiting, leaving empty space
to conjure what happened, make the even truth
a pleasure flow. Child of April 23rd
coming and going, in and out on cue
all parts and ages done by fifty-two.
Vague footprints still in bonds and registers
William Shagspere and *Anne Hathwey* of Stratford,
furnace-sighing lover shotgunned at eighteen:
Susanna; Hamnet, Judith sonne and daughter.
Lost years seeking the bubble reputation,
a name on lists of Bishopgate's petty debtors,
Johannes factotum learning the adrenalin trade
until poor grudger Robert Greene complains
'Trust them not there is an upstart Crow...'
At thirty Hamnet mourned before his teens.
Sudden mentions by poet Drayton and Southwell
and rivals are stealing copies both fair and foul,
now theatre shareholder with friends at court,
wise investor with eyes severe and beard
of frugal cut signing his deals and loans.
A score years, a million dazzling words,
half-dozen lived out a squire at Stratford
and all entailed to Susanna's male heirs,
just a second-best bed as an afterthought
for Anne his wife. Strange will indeed
outriddling Hamlet in riddles left behind.
No one and everyone as each role stares
into the eye and prospect of his soul.
An acorn's ambitious recipe of genes
well sunned and rained unfolds an oak,

nature and nurture scheme with such a will
to soak and breathe all our foibled lives,
a Hamlet echoing every voice around him
who picks bare bones of Plutarch, rakes
over chronicles to fire a brain with plots
he bloods and fleshes, shrewd mood-shifter
luring and juicing a rowdy London yard,
streetwise, no one's fool and yet the fool
in quips and banter glinting his vision's fabric.
There needs no ghost come from his grave
to tell how marrow sweats in every line
as prince, general, lord, queen and thane,
glutton, coward, lecher, soldier, braggart,
every foul-mouthed and calumnious knave,
tramp our patchwork show across the planks.
A long time ago the world began, hey ho!
hey nonny, nonny, o mistress mine!
In how warm a heart do our hearts bask?
Sponge, mimic, scavenger, hustler, clown,
but does the sonneteer occasionally unmask,
allow an actor's visor clatter down?
W.H. onlie begetter's riddle-me-ree
obsession with outwitting time's wrong
thou runnest after that which flees from thee,
so fickle a dark lady and yet to long.
Is passion shaped in pale-blooded veins,
pastmaster in the cold comfort of an art
that dresses hurts while still the self remains
the hidden sum and cipher of every part?
This virtuoso heart that never can unclasp;
All otherness, it slips again beyond our grasp
as each gleaming mood swings on another.
'In youth when I did love,' a grave-digger sings,
Hamlet broods on a thrown-up skull;
Macbeth rinses trembling hangman's hands,
a drunken porter moans his brewer's droop.
Such timing well-graced actor to arrive
and enter at this creaking hinge of history
to strut a glittering stage as Europe wakes
out of a sleepy middle-age to retrace
profaner youth, such flair to tread
the boards in this giant-world of feverish states,

hotbed of new voyages, emissaries and spies,
so barefaced and fancy-free at one
fell swoop to shape and hammer a language,
daring all that Bacon's Latin couldn't dare.
Things dance attendance on fortune's knave,
a talent bursting through as a moment readies,
flawless match of chromosome and chance,
set, props, backdrop every detail
of a plot conspires to cue the lead in
as Burbage lugged his father's lumber to frame
The Globe. As luck would have it the finest
London troupe and a will to hold the mirror up
to what we do, not what we should do,
to tell the story and let it tell itself
with shock and shadow-ironies that peep
between the lines from play to play to hint
at how a knowing voice and unseen eye
that qualms and scruples through soliloquies
still house the sonnets' dreaming realist
applying fears to hope and hope to fears
as from now to how we ripe and ripe.
But did we hear the hint or imagine it?
Greatest mirror, most hidden holder up.

Admiral of Arks

(for Jean Vanier, founder of L'Arche;
born 10 September 1924)

Evacuated from Bordeaux at eleven Vanier
Saw an overloaded captain
Watching a tug of refugees driven away

Whose cries traverse his years and multiply
Among the marred and broken
And fix him with Lazarus's begging eye.

At thirteen as he opts to leave Québec on his own
For Dartmouth's British Naval College,
His army father trusting as though he'd known.

A butterfly collared cadet, chevron winged,
All day moving at the double,
No room for teenagery, tough and Kiplinged;

5 A.M. barefoot scrubbing decks at sea,
Turns below or on the bridge;
Three of his classmates all admirals to be.

A sailor inside sails against the stream.
If you can trust yourself
When all men doubt you. A different dream

As life pulls and loops strands to plot
Surreptitious ins and outs
And tie, as if by chance, the perfect knot.

A concrete asylum where eighty retarded inmates
Tramp their tethered days in circles
Charges his psyche with horror and fascinates.

Whose presence had his friend Père Thomas seen
Crying *I am who I am*
In some noisy muddled sequence of a gene?

To trust the grooves and habitats of love.
Soup, apples from village neighbours.
Raphael and Philippe. One tap and one stove.

Slobber of dailyness. Tasks begun and rebegun.
Small humdrum of the wounded,
Seizures, tears, rushes of anger or affection.

More listening than wanting to do things for,
Fecundity of nothing accomplished,
Ordinary unhurried to and fro of rapport.

No mask or echelons, a kind of upside-downness,
Osmosis of bare and broken
Takers and givers in a single fragile caress.

A flood of middle 1960s volunteers.
Americas, India, Africa, Jerusalem
Flotilla of arks across some forty years.

By guess and by God, fellowships of need,
Ravel decades of care and laughter,
Hurt or seeking minds slowly unmutinied.

Each new community he heartens to adjust,
Admiral of arks, servant-leader,
A father's voice still saying, of course, I trust.

Villagers overlooked, zealous finger-pointings,
Let live of breakage and passage,
And lose, and start again at your beginnings

As after two years' illness his return to hidden
Gradual rhythms of healing that heals,
A stiller brother's keeper who loves unbidden

Guests that might never be if it were known
Chromosome messages had so mistaken.
A refused slab becomes the corner-stone

Lain against the market's coarser grain.
Day by day a giving in
To banalities of love. Over and over again

To announce a vision, even to wear renown
And to fall short anew with every
Ups-a-daisied child let forever down,

A tug still fails all who'll never board.
Yet the joy in Abigail's cry:
To wash the feet of servants of my lord.

The Burning Bush

(for Sigrid Undset, Norwegian novelist,
born 20 May 1882, died 10 June 1949;
awarded Nobel Prize in 1928 for her historical novels
Kristin Lavransdatter *and* Olav Audunssøn*)*

1

A young thing basked on a sunlit slope
in warm Danish earth of infanthood
and clung to Papa, archaeologist back
at last for good and already at two
could list names of Stone Age axes.
Once Papa in a heady moment
allowed his own Sigrid hold
Schliemann's terracotta horse,
a toy a proud child had handled
thousands of miles and years away
in Asia Minor's nine-layered Troy,
that slipped her fickle hands and broke.
Returned to Norway old wine of sagas,
Greek myths and Rome trickle down.
Keeper of finds he'd let her hold
torques and pendants from antique days,
while Mamma, free-minded Dane whet
a daughter's talents with Andersen's tales.
Home now shifted from flat to flat.
Her Papa ails and eleven or almost
Sigrid sat and read aloud
as engrossed he strove to close a work.
By forty he's dead. Barely sixteen
she chose to drop out of her co-ed.
Facts, they'd said, but often no more
than a prop, theory, a kind of try-out,
side-tracks in history's longer light –
her father's Trojan horse of doubt.
Right or wrong, enough is enough,
and Sigrid high horses into the world.

2

Dear Dea, I've sometimes even begun.
Nothing comes right. Burnt on the spot.
I must make art but haven't lived enough.
I think I'm possessed. But if it works or not,
Nothing grips me like this scribbling stuff.
Letters to a Swedish pen-friend, each one
Both dialogue and self-appraisal. *I too*
Want some day to fall in love but my ideal
Is maybe not so high as yours, I only
Want to love and be loved as earthlings do.
Constant passion for what's worldly and real.
Ten years as secretary, a woman lonely
In double life: by day her post; by night
Chaucer, Shakespeare, Byron, Keats, learning
Greek and Latin, Drachmann, Heine, beloved
Sagas. *Dear Dea, I've got only my yearning!*
Mamma worries that she's so late to bed.
The damned office all day, at least I might
Be let do whatever I want at night-time.
A decade breadwinner for mother and younger
Sisters she spent among the office Misses
Who whisper in one-room flats their hunger
For white-horsed knights with infinite kisses,
Dream their dangerous dreams in broken rhyme.
Once we'd authority. Freedom's a colder stone.
Dea, if only we women could be as women are...
Neither to vie or play the cards a man deals.
But has this prophet already seen so far?
Don't marry, Dea, unless head over heels
And sooner hell with him than heaven alone.
Ten years to fumble and open into her voice.
Still the whirl of stubborn genes and hardwire,
Her father's long-sighted perspective squirms
At Hamsun's Pan or Ibsen's selves of choice.
Art's a clamour between our nature and desire,
A crying gap between our angels and worms.
Her first refusal. 'And don't ever bother again
With historical novels. A modern one maybe
You'd never know,' condescends editor Nansen.
Bruised ego she both nurses and disciplines.
So the chic griefs of hapless Marta Oulie:
I've been unfaithful to my husband, she begins.

3

A break and book and a bursary abroad.
At last to Rome where something thawed.
In letters talk of new white blouses,
A black straw hat with roses, carouses
In cheap wine bars until sunrise
And her painter Svarstad, a streetwise
Loner, driven and against the stream,
Shining knight who'd walked her dream.
Happiness is a shooting star, a blitz
To always remember and wish on its
First caresses, still dizzy and new.
I kiss the earth for I never knew
A human could even be this happy
Or if I did it wouldn't ever happen to me.
Rome, Paris, London, Copenhagen.
A kimono. The loveliest I've ever been.
Home, another book and breakthrough.
Married in Antwerp, London for a few
Months, their first-born son in Rome,
And back to Norway to set up home.
A burning bush of temperament needs
To be everything. Mother of feeds
And changes, hostess and author
By night as she worries for a stepdaughter
And son as her husband's ex can't cope.
Painter Svarstad has begun to slope
Off to his atelier and overnight there.
One evening she let down her hair
And wore her olive-green from Rome
But when Svarstad didn't make it home
From a frock that wowed Rome's carousers
She sews for her son a coat and trousers.

4

Separated in the country with children and pets
visits from the step-family she frets about;
her second daughter never quite right,
another son as still by night cigarettes
and caffeine to breathe new lives
Kristin Lavransdatter and Olav Audunssøn,
her passions worn and woven in.

Now more than ever twin strings of genes,
weighted sagas and Danish ballads,
a daughter's double strands laid down
beside a parted helix of two times.
How in a tangle of isms and fragmentation
to find an angle of vision where
love knows no rules and breaks them all
not in a freefall of lone egos
but a knot in a greater story that throws
its light both back and forward to catch
the infinite in flight? Time wears on,
beliefs drift and we think otherwise.
Our human hearts can't shift. O lonely
office girls turn back to before
Enlightenment and yearn for a knight in arms,
give Kristin her head to fall
for a tearaway prince she'd meant to wean
from whim or foolery and shape the one
true cavalier he never was or could be.
Let her ripen strong and humble
to glimpse how from the outset in ecstasy or anger
his ring had bitten in and scarred
her finger or the way a love had underwritten
each fumbled choice, great or small,
undoing all the half-remembered bitter ends.
Light be light, dark dark,
a palette stark and realer set against
fin de siècle anything goes,
chiaroscuro of our consuming doze.
A prophet winding back to stare
forward and finding by retreat and detour
as soil-proud once transgressor
Olav Audunssøn strove to his end to uncoil
inner snakes of clay and blood,
worlds where light and dark interplay

5

A lone figure walks over Brooklyn Bridge.
Her daughter dead, a son shot
Skirmishing Germans in Norway.
Long banned by Nazis, they'd got
Her across to Sweden by sleigh.

Wartime in New York of essays and reportage
And a prophet comes back home wasted,
Her days doubled in nights,
Her life-sum in the red,
A seer with her Trojan hindsight
Whose long perspective watched so far ahead.
Would our sundered dreams of liberty end in tears,
Our broken fellowship
Pondered on a market scales?
Has civilisation begun to slip
As a fabric wears and fails
And a house of progress falls about our ears?
Oracle burdened with too great a convert's zeal,
A third order nun,
A Kristin stumbling to forgive
Those who'd shot her son,
To be, to burn, to live.
Dea, some day to fall in love but my ideal…
Kristin and Olav echo in us and amplify.
Older wine of hindsight,
And yet the bread is new.
Alone into the light,
Burn-out and burning through.
A flaming bush cries *Here am I.*

I've Crossed Famous Rivers

(Ndiwelimilambo enamagama)

(for Nelson Mandela, former President of South Africa, born 18 July 1918)

A slow dripped stone worn by indignities.
No epiphany, revelation, moment of truth
just the long rotten row of African Only.

Die wit man moet altyd baas wes.
The pale man must always be boss.
Die kaffer op sy plek. Nigger in his place.

Rolihlahla, Mandiba, Dalibhunga, Mandela.
Tree-shaker, clan-man, chief à la Bhunga
Russet, white-bellied, stripe-thighed impala

anteloping Africa. *I've crossed famous rivers.*
Less sprinter than long-distance runner coping
boundary by boundary hoping to let both

the bred Thembu kingmaker and royal mentor
first hit his stride as he shed skin by skin,
clan, tribe and stock but also to become

his names for all his people. Tree-shaker,
pathfinder, painstaker, a cross country
pacemaker moving dangerously out ahead.

Even as a boy to win but never to humiliate.
Discipline inscribed in years and genes of grit,
a stubborn smile that seems to begin in an eye

of a student once expelled for making a stand,
a tearaway eluding a planned tribal match,
a gardener of Robben Island sharing among

prisoners and warders his overspill of fruits,
Antigone crying at Creon's unlistening will.
For 28 years never to stand still

Even on the same spot wearing out a shoe
to keep on and on running no matter what.
Talk, plot, debate, argument, growth.

Decades of gestation. A small village boy
he'd whiten his hair with ash in imitation
of his beloved father. Now parent to a nation.

Nkosi sikelel iAfrika. God bless Africa.
Laps of honour in a stadium of success.
Forgiveness. To win but never to humiliate.

Under a frost of grey a wise smile creases.
Yes, to father a country, but to have lost
my children's laughter? *I've crossed famous rivers.*

A Fractured Gleam

(for Mohandas Gandhi,
born 2 October 1869, assassinated 30 January 1948)

1

Detailed, fussy advice to family and ashram:
Avoid spices, cocoa, both tea and coffee;

Figs, raisins, grapes, an orange or a plum,
Home-bread; the clothes to wear, celibacy;

As for ornaments, beware dirt in nose or ears.
I's dotted, *t*'s crossed. A lawyer's ifs and buts.

South Africa a tune-up for 21 years.
'The saint has left our shores,' sighs Smuts,

'I sincerely hope forever.' Yet a personality,
A voice, a humour that captivates. Shy youth

That left become freedom icon in his dhoti,
Mahatma of lifelong experiments in truth.

2

Wire glasses, sandals, bone and loin-cloth
now tipping seven stone of inner strife,
Great Soul of India grown even thinner

than the outcasted unknown London student,
clone English gentleman in a silk top-hat
and his own silver mounted walking-stick.

Violin, French, dancing. Practising alone
from Bell's *Standard Elocutionist* he'd intone
one of William Pitt's high-flown speeches.

It seems as though such shame once sown
must bloom full-blown and wither before
what's overgrown can push for the light.

3

In Gandhi's eyes a glint that won't let go
His wily frame of energy.
So many conflicts in so small a torso.

Frightened boy harassing his child bride,
Minutiae loving dreamer,
A sensuous underlip curbed and denied,

Peacemaker, ascetic gatherer of fame,
Determined hunger-striker
Suffering to atone or gain by stealth his aim?

A drawn line falls short of Euclid's line;
In the so and so of living,
Pure soul and cunning clay combine.

Hopeless visionary and master politico,
Both guru and bargainer
Aware how far to push his quid pro quo

Or so unerringly to choose a perfect token,
Salt and spinning wheel,
Fasts, vows, lockouts or laws broken.

Three times he's called in to broker power,
This maverick of self-rule.
I plough my furrow, I wait my hour.

4

To the hub's eye every spoke is an avenue.
Glamourless persuasion in villages and lanes;
Hindu and Muslim for ages muddled through
Long before an empire's sneaking trains.

One fall and we fall together. All is knit,
As a seed to its tree so our means and ends.
Why banish a tiger to keep a tiger's spirit?
States with bombs are feared even by friends.

Bitter shadow of defeat. A voice is fading.
Remember the salt march to the shore at Dandi?
But round and round a violent souring ring
As a Hindu mob clamours 'Death to Gandhi'.

How can I believe that I alone am right?
The Raj is withdrawing, the stakes are down.
Fragile bird of hope, barely still in flight
Winging out into dark. A seer or clown?

Between two hawks to die a dove for both.
No enemy or failure. One frail humanity.
Toothless foolish sage in his loin-cloth.
Garland him. Feed the lamps with ghee.

5

Gandhi the figurehead useful then as now.
A nation's father or *rishi* crying in vain
Would it have happened as it happened anyhow?
Source, head-streams, feeders, branches, creeks,
On flows the Ganges south across its plain
As water finds the grooves that water seeks.

Hungry the tiger, hungrier still the zealots.
Splits and wars and bomb-poised neighbours.
Though not the tiger, still the tiger's spots.
On flows the river and swings as a river swings,
The more involved, the more the way blurs;
Vision bogged down in the alluvium of things.

Has a globe begun to fear the tiger within?
An ice-cap melting down, our holed ozone.
The hours in prison he'd set aside to spin
And purify just one soul for the sake of all.
To stand against the world though you stand alone.
Mahatma's ghost still teaching green and small

And the views of Jain friend Raychandbhai:
No need to pit extreme against extreme,
The jewel can shine a face for every eye.
To love truth in one glint of a stone,
The live and let live in a fractured gleam.
Lonely Cassandra come into your own.

Whistle-blower

(for Bartolomé de Las Casas, historian, Dominican missionary
and defender of native rights in the Americas;
born Seville [?] 1474, died Madrid 17 July 1566)

1

Young *clérigo* and conquistador on his first escapade
To take Cuba,
Shocked at seeing five hundred of *Los Indos* slayed

But granted land and natives for some years he combines
His heart and gain;
On the make he sends his Indians to work the mines.

Was it a sermon on the feast of Pentecost 1514?
To take away
A neighbour's living is to murder. What does it mean?

Like one who kills a son before his father's eyes
Las Casas *ponders* –
A person who from the gains of the poor offers sacrifice.

A case for native rights once heard from a Dominican
Sinks in
To shake his being and undermine the businessman.

Abandon his Indians? Who'd be kinder than he'd been?
El clérigo hurries
To Governor Velaquez to relinquish his charges and begin

His unheard of mission. The king must halt this disaster;
He boards for Spain.
His peons drudge to their end under another master.

2

Ninety-two years of health and in overdrive;
Some dozen Atlantic crossings and still to outlive

Ferdinand the Catholic, Handsome Philip, Charles V
And even to seem in the end to die at the zenith

Of his growth. Several lives in the breath of one:
Voyager, trader, radical, priest, historian.

A merchant's son with his Salamanca degrees,
By twenty-four he'd sailed with Columbus to the Indies,

So mission after mission between dominions and capital
Reformer determined to serve even in his shortfall.

For over three decades he travels to challenge king,
Cardinal or chancellor who just as they're enacting

Change will die. Endless buck-passing juntas
That kill with kindness or are rigged by Bishop Burgos.

Campaigner destined to fail even in his success
As every ban on slaves he cajoles Madrid to pass

The conquerors somehow override and undermine.
Shuttle apostle both catching and missing the boat.

3

Eight years of mid-life withdrawal
To a Dominican close, he has to refrain
From preaching. Days of study to renew
'The state of his soul'. Outside the wall
Cortes is conquering New Spain,
Alvarado Guatemala, Pizarro Peru.

A hate figure settlers now rejoice
To see ensconced and out of the way,
A troublemaking son of a gun.
In worlds of turmoil a lone voice,
Doubts cracking in his vessel of clay:
Perhaps he wasn't the chosen one?

Necessary methods must sometime hurt.
Better such modern means for reaching
Infidel so long as he comes to believe.
(Apostles had miracles up their sleeve.)
Conquest so much quicker than preaching;
Fill them with terror or else they revert.

To peach on his own? Nothing lower!
To win their slaves they'd marched
Months across uncharted terrain,
Toiled and bled. A small gain
For weeks frozen, starved, parched.
Boat-rocker. Whistle-blower.

Civilisations, plants, animals, lands,
Realms of discovery whirl by,
Unknown gold or precious stone.
To save a people and redeem his own?
Strands he'd so wanted to tie
Keep on slipping out of his hands.

African slaves play on his mind,
Mistakes made, his failed colony
Journeys to force Pizarro to cease
Terror called him or had he pined
For action? In Guatemala his plea
To take the feared Tuzutlan by peace.

4

Old mocking cliché:
'Try it', they said, 'Try with words only
And sacred exhortation'.
Clérigo and brethren
Are learning Quiché.

A people who'd once known
Cities, temples, pyramids, palaces,
Stars and warriors' fame
Written by hieroglyph,
Sculpted in stone.

Refusing the party line
Again Las Casas insists on trust,
Tiny inflections of tact,
Slow grammar of respect
To conjugate and decline

Madness of hundreds massacred
As easy grindstones for Spanish swords,
Bad faith of slavery,
Trinkets, wine, bribes
And their broken word

As conquistadors leave
Yet another cruel hierograph
Inscribing the earth with greed.
Ask the Mayan dead
Do stones grieve?

Over four and a half
Centuries and poet Ak'abal
From Totonicapán
Writes what might have been
Las Casas' epigraph.

Guatemala laments:
Ri ab'aj man e mem
Taj xa kakik'ol ri kich' awem
Not that the stones are dumb,
They hold their silence.

Unbroken

(for Máirtín Ó Cadhain, Irish novelist and short story writer, born 1906, died 18 October 1970)

Fiery Cois Fhairrge teacher from a rugged line
Of storytellers,
Dismissed for his politics from his school post,
Interned in the Curragh at thirty-three,
Teaching other metal hut dwellers
Irish and spreading his wings: Ó Cadhain
Of Tintown Academy.

Tolstoy, Dostoyevsky, Gogol, Chekhov, Gorky,
Europe's extremes
Flirting in his busy head:
I'm learning Russian for all I'm worth.
His letters hungry for word of friends
And gossip, short stories begun, schemes
For novels, a stubborn humour, quirky
And down-to-earth.

Book after book pored over and underlined.
But how to undo
History? Our island as it ought
To have been. A dark road indeed.
A windswept tree bends to renew
And graft centuries of Europe's thought;
A vision of two worlds combined,
Few may heed.

Two long parted strands tied in a node
Of frail dream
As the wind whines in stone
Walls and tells again in a gritty,
Nasal voice stories to redeem
An unbroken line who fingers to bone
Worked their life and tramped the road
To Bright City.

Burden of being both outside and within:
To count the cost
Because you've walked beyond,
To know the loss because you grew
Inside and feel so double-crossed
By your own who still can't respond
To your dream. Has the weave begun to thin
Unable to renew?

All the scattered energy beating the air,
Epistles or protests
Or scolding follies of the blind.
Can no one see? Will nothing halt
This unravelling? A tongue invests
Two thousand years to haunt the mind;
So rich a cloth so soon threadbare,
Fraying by default.

'Have you heard,' he glows, *ag déanamh na gcosa*
'A newborn foal *trying to find its feet?*'
His urge to include everything he'd heard,
Burrowing deeper to embrace a whole
Planet. Dried cowpats used for peat
In Aran that Tolstoy knew from Russia;
A globe inferred.

Under a cocky Rabelaisian carapace,
Tilt and wag
And his craggy snorting laugh
The bones of some story in the making
As he recalls lives that seem to nag
For words he plucks from history's riff-raff.
Behind a stern and pouting face
A heart is breaking.

WOUNDED MEMORY

Της λύπης είναι τέμενος η γη.
Αγνώστου πόνου δάκρυ στάζει η αυγή·
αι ορφαναί εσπέραι αι χλωμαί πενθούσι·
και ψάλλει θλιβερά η εκλεκτή ψυχή.

Earth is a sanctuary of sorrow.
Dawn drops a tear of unknown pain;
the wan orphan evenings mourn
and the select soul intones sadly.

CAVAFY
translated by Rae Dalven

Bushmen

1

Thousands of years they wander lands lush
With wild game and berries,
Nomads in Africa's southern veldt and bush,

Chattering bands of hunters and gatherers at ease
With how a cosmos behaves.
Short, apricot-skinned, eyes like the Chinese,

Come-day-go-day Bushman paints or engraves
An unbroken story in red
Ochre figures across the walls of the caves;

From Drakensberg north to the Zambezi the bled
Eland and hunter obsessed
And tall in ecstasy reaches for his Great Godhead.

Alone before the Bantu squeezed them north-west
To the Kalahari, before
Paintings of galleons and Dutch farmers expressed

Forebodings, still they dance a stalking metaphor,
The Masawara and San
Big in their trance as dreaming upwards they adore.

2

Around the fire they tend
Women clap up a chant and rhythm,
On a verge of trance
Dancers dance on,
Flux
Of buttocks
And ankle-rattlers prattle and hum

As the sweated spirit's *n/um*,
Great God's sap rising to the boil
With yelps of *qai! qai!*
'Pain,' they cry out,
Rush
And push
Helter-skelter to the edge while

Stars and Bushmen reconcile
Their oneness in this dance they weave
And lay their hands to heal.
The sacred eland eaten,
Praise
The prey's
Own surrender to lend its life.

The surrounding dark is rife
With bawdy shrieks as a medicine man
Out on a limb stalls
And falters in his shivering
Dance,
His trance
Too deep willy-nilly he's lain

Beside the fire to regain
His mind. A kinship mends its dissonance
In this frenzy of togetherness;
Things done undone, every
Drift
Or rift
Healing in a hell-for-leatherness of dance.

3

Centuries of cross-purpose, claim and counter-claim:
They fence and graze where ancestors hunted game;
Poison arrowed Pygmies we never managed to tame.

Around the edges of farms, armies, factory or mine
Diseased or lost or absorbed by default or design,
The tattered remnants of natives brought into line.

4

A dream that dreamed the Masawara's
Stars peters out. Some strays endure
Underlings in a Kalahari game enclosure.
What's gone a dumb-show,
Mourn what was to become in all that was.

A broken twig, how grass stems were bent,
The call of a bird, even the shape of a spoor
Itself, the sacred eland's delicate signature
Touching the benign earth,
Whispered signs or hand messages sent

Along millennia. And then a line drawn
In the sand, the life-thread someone loaned
For a while and passed on. Nothing owned.
Firewood fetched by a wayside
Camps pitched at sunset, broken at dawn.

Dance for our healing, dance for falling rain
As greedy boreholes dry up the water-table.
O Cain, o Cain you murder brother Abel!
The Bushmen's shadows thin,
Poison arrows of shame have hit the vein.

Hyenas howl, the eye of the lioness glints,
Upright fall and stars shoot down the sky.
Hair on our heads are clouds when we die.
Praise names of our God lost,
Wind makes dust to take away our footprints.

Blizzard

(dedicated to Roman Vishniac and Eva Hoffman)

1

Teaming, quarrelsome, noisy world of *shtetl*,
and ghetto, raucous melancholy of klezmer,
once scattered across Europe's eastern plains

the Russian born American Roman Vishniac
hurried to snap a last exposure to the light,
his lens shuttering lovingly each gesture of life:

shopkeepers, housewives, girls hungry to live,
milkman, printer, cattle-trader, stamp-collector,
Talmudic scholar in his fur hat and muffler,

cobbler, watchmaker, barber, second-hand dealer,
women gossiping with buckets at a vendor's door,
an elder stroking his beard in the *Beth Midrash*,

the salesman carrying his bags to the rail station,
a man saw in one hand, his *tallith* in the other,
as dark figures in caftans bend into the snow,

Rabbi, cantor, tailor, peddler and beggar,
young men gathering to dream of Palestine,
a rapt Hasid walks along a swarming street,

where a merchant haggles over the price of a hen,
someone is inviting the local fool for dinner,
children are queuing up outside the *mikva*,

and *cheder* boys swat under the eye of a *melamed*,
a *yeshiva* student brushes his coat for the Sabbath
And a father fits his son with a cap for the blizzard.

2

Since Babylon in wandered Europe,
A nestling presence among not of,
Hunkering down and chequering in.

Cossacks, Turks, Swedes, Prussians.
Remember one side will win –
Watch well the way the winds blow!

Mystic, carnal dangerous other
But some *pogromchik* is lying low.
No hatred but we always knew

Side by side until the crunch.
Sorer still that Jew betrays Jew.
We shared sweet fellowship in God's

House. Two thousand years among
The *Goyim.* Together and at odds.
Bitter sigh between two sighs.

3

Shtetlekh seething with long quarrels of change,
Zionists, *Balabutim*, Marxists or Hasidim,

Tug and pull of custom and sudden challenge.
Some dreamers of *golden medina* cross to grim

Lower East Side sweat
shops beyond the Hudson.
O don't look for me where streams are playing,

O sukh mikh nit vu fontanen shpritsn
You will not find me there. Others are staying

To argue the toss of progress with endless fever
Of *Yashiva* students searching every midrash

For whatever meaning might still hide, whatever
Might yet have become before the hour of ash,

Before the looted sanctuary, the broken ark,
The silent klezmer. In a dumb fallen prayer

Their stubble glares like buckwheat after dark.
Don't look for me. You will not find me there.

4

A Pole in Brańsk stumbles on grave-slabs with Hebrew
Nazis used to pave a lane and flags some hid,
Unheeded whetstones in barns or sheds he'll now bring
To where the Jewish graveyard was. Curiosity
becomes in time a sombre gesture of remembrance.

A ruddy sheepskinned leather-booted farmer's witty
'They'd cheapen for Christmas' sort of shrew boy the Yid
Remark of one who'd once carted to graves a slew
Of dead. 'If that's what they want, you can't say a thing'
Even a sigh and sense of let-up, a jovial good riddance.

'Noisy as a *cheder*,' they still half-consciously repeat.
A scatter of Jewish words remain – the gone within,
A trace of woven *us* and *them*. The *Goy* and Jew.
'Richer but they too had their poor ones, *oy*, they did.
But one becomes used to people. I feel their absence.'

They are only truly dead who've been forgotten.
'Yes,' agrees another, 'I grew up on this street
As I walk here I recall exactly who lived where:
Shapiros, Gottliebs, Goldwasser, Tykocki and in
The next house that man, what was his name, the one

Who did business with my Papa?' Once thick and thin
Of side-by-sideness slowly fades. The Gemora knew
To kill a human is to kill a whole world, to cheat
Them of all their children's children unbegotten.
A questioning prayer in the long anguish of a *shofar*.
Master of the Universe, why? O what have you done?

Palestine

1

On walls of Gaza City's government building
Someone wrote Vegetius's Roman words:
Let him who desires peace prepare for war.

General stickler and armchair conqueror
Whose fourth century treatise undergirds
Every ruler's feet of rubble, gilding

Electric shocks and grillings used to keep
Mistrust at bay with supergrass or mole,
Intelligence and of course security for all.

Barak or Mukhabarat. And will we fall
And fall into Vegetius's blackest hole?
Walls that never talk must sometimes weep.

2

A handcuff drawn around an Arab substate
Glow-eyed martyrs dodge to freight a bomb.

Black and white of slowly simmered hate,
Another busload blown to kingdom come.

That Jews again should board a bus to die?
But now missiles fired to take a suspect out.

Each cold revenge of eye for eye for eye
And so this grieving turn and turn about.

The *saheed* wafted straight to paradise,
Sweet juices drunk to fête the newly sainted

But cameras watch the tell-tale swollen eyes
Of mothers wailing over their lonely dead.

This endless blindfold ring of anger vent.
Abraham's children pitch their mourning tent.

3

Abraham, Ivreham, Isdud, Ashdod,
Names that name a double vision,
Yibne and Yavne, Lydda and Lod.

Two millennia remembering Israel:
And she called the child Ichabod –
The glory of Israel gone, a frail

Look back at freighted golden days
Like some fondled childhood detail
Of vanished ghettos, yearning gaze.

Broken neighbours, prey to zealots,
Routed villagers, history's strays
Squat in camps or shacks, have-nots

In fruitless alleyways where men
In djellabas talk of figs and apricots,
Dream of villages, dream of then…

Foolish blood of right or wronging
Things gone that never come again.
Is every memory another longing?

Two rootholds grope the shifting sand
With all the tears of sweet belonging.
Two memories in vowels of one land.

Shalom and Salaam unreconciled.
Solomon takes his sword in hand.
Cry out wise mothers of the child.

4

Two separated domains cut-off and brought to their knees.
Backgammon clacks as youths throw stones on the street.
Another permit that comes too late to visit dying kin,
A student thwarted, a pass withdrawn and ends won't meet;
At check-points trucks of fresh cut flowers wilt in delays,
Some minor Vegetius busy nipping hope in the bud,
Squeezed by settlers, gridirons of asphalt highways

Until their promised land becomes this no-win zone
Where victims fall in love with raging victimhood.
Day by day a gift of bread has turned to stone.
How, then tell me, can we make peace with Israelis?
Now another border closure to seal their anger in.

Is that Arab beside you preparing to pull the pin?
If our side loses of course the other will score.
Grind of *qui vive*, relentless doubt, suppressed fear.
Another suicide bomber shadows across a door.
Pizzeria, hotel, party disco, market, bus
And again today someone's lover's body sack.
We give them everything and look how they betray us.
Too long burdened victimhood, a haunted Jew
Too laden still and too intent on hitting back
To learn the stronger's generous move, derring-do
To stop the dizzy spiral, a giant too keen to win,
Samson bringing pillars down around his ears.

Layer on layer of yellow sandstone myth and years,
Hill of Zion, Mount of Olives, Dome on the Rock,
City of yearning and broken bread, city of *Salaam*
Somewhere once you dreamed a peace beyond the flock,
Shalom of ripe commingling and let-live mosaic
Of all the thriving clamour of eastern streets and smells,
Coffee, *falafel*, *halva*, deals with upfront money,
Al Quds sunning itself in noise of give and take.
Old city of *muezzins*' calls, chants and swinging bells
The savour of your soil delights my mouth like honey.
Your Western Wall so full of slotted prayers and tears.
O fragile city! Jerusalem. Our earthly Jerusalem.

5

And so another road to Jerusalem loops both back and beyond.
Whose are still the voices where the past and future correspond?

Poet Aharon Shabtai like Amos dresser of the sycamore tree
Cries out *my lips mutter: Palestine! Do not die on me!*

A creature born of our people's love will burst forth into the blue.
Listen, his heart is beating through mine – I'm a Palestinian Jew.

Whirlwind, earthquake, then, fire. But even in the end you find
The stiller smaller voice. At last Elijah is learning to unwind.

O Abraham, could you not bear the fire-worshipper a single night?
As mystic Rumi's *cavernous shadows need the light to play*

And light alone can lead you to the light, so too, so too
Each soul will know what it has done and what it has failed to do.

The evening dove's olive leaf and the chatter under the palm.
Abraham, Ishmael, Isaac, Jacob and the tribes. Shalom! Salaam!

Doggone Blues

1

Home, village, tribe. Uprooted
Centuries of men and women
Chained, shipped, sold, branded.

First dim recall of Guinea.
No name or date. Master's
Jim, Esther, Ned or Jenny.

The lucky ones maybe roost
As cooks or house-slaves,
Few learn trades or crafts; most

From the day a child lifts a hoe
To work the fields until they
Drop between shafts of a plough.

Some drivers humane, some mean
And any spirit shown
Whipped until they're broken in.

We bake de bread, dey gib us de cruss
Wails the juba beater,
We sif de meal, dey gib us huss.

Nobody whose trouble nobody knows.
Crooned endurance in song
A story waiting to erupt in Blues.

2

So many "head of slaves" to tend the crop this year.
To buy a breeder and maybe bide until she mates.

The young man rides up, beckons the watching overseer
And says send me Juno or Missylene or Chlory
And then rides on into the trees, dismounts and waits

Or a young housemaid taken and soon set in pillory,
A wife's jealous cuffs and whippings sting the bone.

Quadroon, octoroon, their careful measures of mulatto.
Of course, give a coon an inch and he'll take a mile.
When you ain't got nobody you can call your own.

They'll take over the place. Yes, sir, we know Sambo!
And guilt stalks. Old shadowy nigger in the wood-pile.

3

Civil war. Then the Day of Jubilo
And slaves who still didn't know
Quite why? Tears on either side:
Owner and bondsman. Tongue-tied
Uncertain Blacks crowd a gateway,
A mind to leave, a mind to stay.
An' when your stomach's full o' slack
Some come begging to be taken back,
Others go stumbling on to die
On highways. *Brother, don't you cry!*
Saw-mills cotton-gins, lumber-camps,
Levee-banks, floods, glades, swamps.
Ought's an ought. Figger's a figger.
All for de white man, none for de nigger,
Sharecroppers rub your sleepy eyes,
Another slavery in another guise.
Started at the bottom, I stayed right there,
Don't seem like I gonna get nowhere.
Sourgraped South still juggles laws,
Klan lynchings or grandfather clause,
A Black finger as a pickled momento.
Who'd like a daughter to marry a Negro?
A ruse by any name to do them down.
Going to leave this Jim Crow town…
North, where they think money grows on trees
Don't give a doggone if ma black soul freeze.
Pittsburgh, Cleveland, St Louis, Chicago
No heaven on earth, Lord, wherever I go.
Nobody's nobody, a margin survivor,
Mule-skinner, rambler, steel-driver,

Convict, logger, pimp or whore,
Outsider, railroader, stevedore,
Boomer, number-runner, bootlegger.
First of 'twenty and odd negers'
Black Anthony Johnson steps down
From 'a man of warre' at Jamestown
The year of grace 1619.
All these years where have you been
Dogtrot cabin to shanty and slum?
Was it Fulani? But they left you dumb.
Flat-talk, dog-Latin, gumbo or jive,
An endless lust just to stay alive,
Migrant, loafer, roustabout.
All odds on a whiting out.
A chattel bought, a chattel sold,
Nobody's nobody's story told
In mumble, holler, scat or groan
Go tell 'em ivories how to groan.

4

Let everybody know the trouble I know.
A summer march to Washington King led:
We shall overcome August banners stream.

Before they overcome they shall undergo
Glower or backlash grudge of privilege shed.
Court by court a hard-etched self-esteem.

The sniper's rage is somewhere lying low.
But how to heal the white to love instead?
The preacher man calls out *I have a dream.*

For angry young an Uncle Tom too slow.
O black is beautiful! The Panther is dead
Or somewhere gone to ground in academe.

So the stalemate breadline snare of ghetto,
Gangs and drugs, lives hung by a thread,
Bias bound and hemmed invisible seam

Of half-forgotten scar and hickory blow.
The master's shadow falls years ahead:
Every lash and backlash a burden to redeem.

Turn about and wheel about, jump Jim Crow.
Satchmo, go bugle up the marching dead.
A ghost preacher cries *I still have a dream.*

Remember

1

Remember a long Armenian summer without dawn,
April 1915 to September 22.
Death cried for ravens and ravens darkened Van.

Young Turks tap on doors and Madame Hagopian
Hurries to hide her son in a mulberry tree
As ten thousand bodies float in Lake Geoljik.

Tricked and gathered. An *Ausrottungspolitik* –
Policy of elimination – a German diplomat reports
(Who'll later die for Hitler's bungled coup).

Behind the Great War's veil the soldiers slew
Or drowned thousands a day. Litany of slaughter:
Van, Trebizond, Bitlis, Sivas, Kharput.

For some a stoked up envy, a chance to loot;
For many old cooped and brooded neighbour hate,
Abdul the Damned's contempt again overt.

Women and children over mountain desert,
Stripped naked, preyed upon and abused.
As vultures hover above the roadside dead.

Crawling, maimed, starved, begging for bread
But south to a Mesopotamia most never reach,
A trail of rifle-butted shrieks and wailings.

Asia Minor black with ravens' wings
A million and a half Armenian dead before
The mulberry sheds the leaves of seven seasons.

2

A people's homeland for over three millennia.
Then word leaks out of slaughter in Armenia.

Their German allies hear but will see no evil.
A muted protest. Let nothing cause upheaval.

Waves of sympathy. Compassionate well-to-do
Funnelling millions of kindness dollars through.

'The broad interest of humanity', says poet Pound.
Woodrow Wilson pads the softer middle-ground.

A cruel and merciless fate. Our words' slippage.
Editorials. Press reports and months of coverage.

The carrions rage across the blotted sky.
And in the bitter end the world stands by.

3

Under the soot-winged ravens
a torch. Brave Mary Louise
Graffam, missioner from Maine,
only alien to refuse to leave
Armenians from Sivas on their
deportation southward march
toward the Euphrates valley,
witness to how Turk and Kurd
(men already lured and dead)
robbed, beat, raped, kidnapped.
Everyone who lagged behind
killed... I saw hundreds of them.
Some died of thirst; others
went crazy. Like the rest,
I was all in rags. On the run
one end of the camp to the other.
Forbidden by the local mutessarif
to pass on beyond the Euphrates
she watches her pupils file across.
Back in Sivas to tend orphans
underground aid, food smuggled
to mountain caves, trials for treason.
Thousands saved or alleviated;
above all an unflinching witness:
we kept carbolic acid on window

sills to keep the odour of dead
from coming in. There were
hosts of dogs feeding on bodies.
The sky was black with birds.

4

A drape of ravens flap their bitter wings.
Sleight-of-hand order, double directive,
Ceremonial secret oaths, sniggered codings:
'Departed convoy', 'provide with bread and olive'.
Deceit of trenches, diggers despatched on the spot.
Infants choked by steam, mad doctors, nightmare
Deportations (males or stragglers to be shot)
Long wasteland caravan, cortège to nowhere.
And who remembers the Armenian genocide?
Quadrupled blueprint, Hitler's upscaled *Vorbild.*
Of eighty two Terpandjians, eighty died:
Grandfather, father, mother, brothers killed.
Megerditch, Garabet, Touma, Shukri, Paul;
A name for each three hundred thousand to recall.

Fall-out

(after John Hersey's Hiroshima)

1

Island by island, Guam, Okinawa. To stun
Them to surrender sooner. To cast the die.

Cross-legged Dr Fujii read his *shinbun*
As widow Nakamura stood watching by

Her window a neighbour who'd now begun
Tearing down his house so he'd comply

With new defence fire-lanes and everyone
Wondered when and what? Three planes fly

Over before the all-clear sounds. None
Who'd survive that morning knew just why

A step this way or that had meant they'd won
What others lost. Imagine one step awry?

Enola Gay unloads. Below the August sun
Broad Island's hundred thousand woke to die.

A pilot logs: *My God, what have we done?*
Wounds of light enrage the hush of sky.

2

On pavements they retch, wait death and die.
Quiet ungrudged passing. All for the country.
Emperor, ten thousand years! Vive Majesty!
Tennō-Heika. Banzai! Banzai! Banzai!
Sudden fires rage out of the queasy murk.
All day still-living wander to Asano Park.

Maples, laurel, pines still green and upright
By rock-pool gardens. In the shades caress
Widow Nakamura's sick brood sleepless
With excitement. Her son sees with delight
A gas storage tank torching the night air.

Faces erased by flash burns are calling out
Mizu! Water! As Tanimotosan fumbling
His basin of water over corpses, stumbling
Apologies to the dead, relieves their drought.
Mizu! Mizu! One man takes and drinks,
Raises himself slightly, bows and thanks.

Then bloated drops of rain trounce the soil.
Out of a blazing city's convection swirls
Of angry uprooted trees a funnel hurls
Débris winding high in the air a coil
Of iron roofs and doors. Eerie whirlwind.
Takakurasan shields his feebler friend.

Dr Sasaki, of thirty the sole unharmed
Among medics, dazed begins to roam
A broken hospital dabbing Mercurochrome;
Overcome by injured hordes that swarmed
To him, he wiped, daubed, bound and tended.
A hundred thousand either doomed or dead.

City of woe, scorched back to its bones.
Four square miles of red-brownish scar,
Crumpled bicycles, shells of tram or car,
Mica traces fuse in granite gravestones.
The lingering slough off their clammy skin;
The silent nurse a silent wounded gene.

3

Widow Nakamura's ten years
penury as no one
wants the maimed left-overs.

Schoolgirls out to clear fire lanes
disfigured rejects
sent to New York for touching up.

Tanimoto's daughter Koko
a jilted fiancée
deemed too smitten by fall-out.

Beta particles, gamma rays,
lurking scars,
purple spots of leukaemia,

Broken wall of foetus cells'
strange aberrations,
stunted or skull-shrunk in womb.

Hibakusha. Outcast. Bomb-touched.
Victims' victims.
Sentence handed down in chromosome.

4

As only days after it fell the hidden
Roots of organs roused began to climb
Above the ground before their time

Lush over ashes and wreckage unbidden
Sickle-senna, morning glories and bluets
Purslane, clotbur, goosefoot, Spanish bayonets

Wound the charred trees or anxious weed
Tangled gutters, roofs and fallen stones
To bloom wildly among the city's bones,

A million and a half so quickly now succeed –
After forty years one in ten survivors –
In this phoenix town of sybarites and strivers,

Of geisha houses, coffee shops and brothels,
Leaf-lined avenues chock-a-block with cars,
Born again in baseball and neon lighted bars.

Green pine trees, cranes and turtles…
Widow Nakamura sings once more in May
At flower festivals for the Emperor's birthday

As Toshio, her son, who never can forget
The fire, before dawn commutes once again
By train to golf with his useful businessmen

And an older Dr Sasaki harbours the regret
That he couldn't label all the unearthed dead.
What nameless souls still hover unattended?

Eclipse

1

A myth of no losers, no few,
No inner other or need to warrant
Rights of tongue or belief.
Who has ever heard of Ainu?

Land of rising sun. Hokkaidō,
Honshū, Shikokū, Kyushū.
One seamless folk,
Archipelago of Yamato.

Hokkaidō? North Coast Road,
Renamed and annexed Ezo
Island of Ainu stock
Whose ways slowly erode.

Pioneers, missions, uneven trade.
Kindred of matriliny, node
And lattice of mores undone,
Their native gods renege

Who once steered the Kurile chain,
Sakhalin, Honshū. Origin vague,
But homeland for two millennia
Before the Meiji legerdemain

Surnamed and labelled them *dojin*
'Natives', surveyed the whole terrain
Changing place names to their own.
A blotting out. A sucking in.

2

By nineteen hundred two thirds extinct. The moral,
Smiles a law-maker over his smiling table,

By irresistible force of nature, a superior wins,
Our nations duty to cure misfortunes of indigenes.

Prudent givers and takers, fishers and hunters
At pains to dispatch the souls of slaughtered bears

To heal the earth's sweet gifting wound.
Everything borrowed. Nothing ever owned.

The sphere of living, the sphere of gone or unborn
A seamless globe where dead in dreams return.

Their Ekishi leaders chosen to be open-handed,
Lavish keepers of nature, begin to trade

Their prey for sugar, clothes or sake and lacquers
To assuage their gods who turn unhearing ears.

Unwillingly they turn to farm bad land and fail.
Kindly, simple-minded, stupid, slothful. A nail

That's sticking up will be hammered down.
Nothing borrowed. Everything must be owned.

A light denied. A planet moves in between.
Two crossing globes of meaning. One unseen.

3

Nineteen eighties and an Ainu
Fell for a girl in Tanikawa.
When parents balked they knew
She had to elope. Petty bourgeois

Shame declares a daughter dead.
In Nibutani school a master
Complains the Ainu smell. Rounded
Eyes, a beard that grows faster.

School drop-outs. Mostly jobless.
Some in summer revive rites
For tourists, show wares and dress.
Some just incognito urbanites.

More Japanese than Japanese.
In willed absorption a double
Loss: neither those nor these.
Gods forsaken still untouchable.

4

In eclipse peoples saw a body dying,
A darkened planet overcome,
A lamp obscured, a globe shadowed.

Old need for an upper hand. What glowed
Snuffed under another's thumb.
Outshone star. A by-thing.

Ishikaribetsu, o greatly meandering
River once sacred to the Ainu
Describe your arc south and westward

To tell a forgotten name, a lost word.
No standing still. Grieve a residue
Swept along by history's slandering

Winners, mourn at every turn strewn
Kinships, lines waning or scored
Through. The map-wiped Ainu.

Solar goddess Amaterasu
Has raised her grass-mower sword.
A risen sun deletes the moon.

Outposts

1

Capricious Queen Bess insisting that she'd learn
To greet her foreign guests in kind
Had ordered her own primer of the Irish tongue

And cast a special font to spread among
The people books to teach reforms
For fear they'd choose Spain's Popish sway.

Vous êtres le gentilhomme de bonne qualité?
Quality. Calen o custure me!
Henry V's Pistol mocks French with gibberish.

Or was Shakespeare aware that this was Irish:
Cailín ó Chois tSiúire mé –
'I'm a girl from River Suir side, a melody

Borrowed for A sonet of a louer for a lady
And sung at the end of eurie line
The original *Calen o castureme*!

But Edward Spencer's scorning throw-away
The bards which are to them as poets
Sows his seed of doubt that blooms as shame.

2

Nothing else but to make way by the blood of army
To enlarge their territories of power and tyranny;
That is an unlawful war, a cruel and bloody

Work...that the cause of the Irish native in
Seeking their just freedoms... Leveller Walwyn
Appeals before the Cromwell wars begin

In earnest...*is the very same as our cause here.*
Eoghan Rua of Tyrone back from Spain in the year
1642, a strategist they fear,

European *extraordinaire* and after Benburb
All but Dublin at his feet, when Roundheads curb
His power by terror. *To hell or Connacht* a proverb.

Driven from their proper, natural, native rights.
Cassandra-like Walwyn has the future in his sights
But no one cares. No one steers by his lights.

3

Thinned and broken by famine,
a scramble to shed the past;
teacher and parent connive:
for any Irish word a score
on a stick hung from the neck,
a slap for every notch.

To seem to move with the times.
Children reared to leave
and Mother Church's myth
how clearly it's God's will
that they'd embrace English
to bring the faith abroad.

A new state's doers soon
blind-eye a weary dream.
Report on report. Schemes
keep the show on the road.
A handful of honest souls
swim against the tide.

Still silly season letters
preserving a native tongue
or outbursts of self-loathing
they talk through their erse.
Cell doubling of self-doubt.
A tally stick in the mind.

Meanwhile school playground
by playground a balance shifts.
Household by single household.
Against seas of erosion
A few limpets of hope.
A cling of scattered outposts.

4

A TV documentary on Irish in Tyrone
With archived voices from the Sperrins
Outlying vestiges. Lingering aberrance
Here and there on a hill's spur.
Raised by a grandmother, alone
Seán Ó Caireallláin in a stony redoubt;
Páidí Láidir left with a sister,
Loners and odd ones out.

Sound bytes direct from Caisleán Glas:
Dreas 'a bout', 'a turn', 'some'
With its middle vowel a pet idiom.
A final eavesdrop. Fading noise
Of a dialect sinks in the dross
And waste of things as Sperrins' limestone
Caps hold their glacial poise
Over Tír Eoghain. Land of Eoghan.

An interviewed professor's explanation
How such communities erode:
Protestant minister, the main road,
A lame teacher who'd forced English,
The Board of Education,
A priest's *stop your gibberish*
And talk your proper language!

A young woman learner talking
In her parents' tavern
With a mountain man who'd return
To his shieling with a week's supplies.
Gaelic Leaguers bring
Their song and dance and medals won.
An afterglow they want to lionise
Until one by one by one....

Language's frail brinkmanship
Before it falls. Something age-old
Slips, lets go its last foothold.
Closing footage. The mood alters
A fraction as a cheerful clip
Of a bird-like voice lifts a song
A bar or two before she falters
Into English. *I forget...*

Crying out

1

Griefs written in wounded memories' song
Wind across our centuries saying no
To any easiness of why the world is wrong,

Irreversible lines of ordeals once borne
In sudden flattened notes, a long slow
Uncoiling strain of losses we need to mourn.

O don't look for me where streams are playing –
In sweatshops' *klezmer* a *shtetl*'s long ago.
No soft-pedalling such musics of belonging,

This knowing in the marrow how crops can fail –
Fair hills of Erin, *Bánchnoic Éireann óighe* –
Some coffin-ship is busy setting its sail.

There behind the jazz a soul is keening –
No heaven on earth, Lord, nowhere I go –
Holding open all our agonies of meaning.

2

The long mute pleas of the dead
For us to remember things
So beyond our ken we barely control

Our deepest urge to shun in dread
Their clammy-handed nobblings,
To flee the ghostly buttonhole

Of those whose testimony shocks
Too much for us to hear.
Of patterns we're destined to rehearse

Unless a patient listening unblocks
Such clogged up fear
Of our histories' ancient mariners,

Voyages we need to face and word,
Stories of dreams still-born,
Tragedies that never found a voice,

Cries of agony yet to be heard.
So much we must mourn
Until our broken bones rejoice.

3

A history of our world unravels into histories,
The crying out of our once forgotten stories,

The mended reed of voices we've refound
Proclaiming all that was trampled underground.

But out of our darkest silences now instead
We risk becoming everything we dread:

The fractured clamour of each remembering victim
As deaf to the world as the world was once to them.

Given too many memories our psyche smothers.
Will our victimhood learn to keep this word for others?

4

Habits of mind reassure,
a sleepwalking that gradually turns its face
against the angel of change,

a slow silting up,
encrustations of recall, our deadwood,
long cortège of tradition

as the stare of stone icons,
remindings of misfortune inscribed in place
or mute testimonies of vestige.

How can we shift our gaze
to leave what has been, the *déjà vu*, the before,
and dare to spring the trap?

Memory, mother of muses,
wake us, shake us up out of this haunted
past that will not pass.

5

As we choose a friend
In the end
We blend or select memories to mend
Whatever engine moves
Our spirits on,

But don't efface
The place
Or trace of any lost or wounded face
Stained with its loves and lives
From our horizon.

Still we recall
The fall
Of all behind the gossamer wall.
Or when the thimbled bells of foxgloves
Summon the gone

We won't forget
Our debt.
And yet
To allow a spring night let
Slip our sleepless doves
Into the dawn.

ANGEL OF CHANGE

Who has not found the Heaven – below –
Will fail of it above –
For Angels rent the House next ours,
Wherever we remove –

EMILY DICKINSON

Overview

Giddy world of shuffle and hotchpotch
Criss-cross planet of easy mix and match.

Keyboards tap a galaxy of satellites
And monies shift in nervous kilobytes

Across a grand bazaar of cyberspace.
Migrants roam our busy market-place.

Noise and anguish of an age. Free-range.
Freewheeling. Nothing endures but change.

Given a globe where borders leak and flow
A violin pleads beside a sitar and koto

As nightly starving Sudanese now stare
Out of the tube. And no hiding unaware

Or folding out again an old cocoon.
No turning back. We've reached the moon.

Adam, atom-splitter, rider in space.
Is this our earth's frail and wispy face?

Hovering

We've seen how wisps of cloud scud
The face of the earth
Over such furrows of soil and blood,
Wrinkled maps of shifts and moves,
The lineaments of nationhood.

Gone the musket dream and bayonet,
Now our fusion
Weaponry, our Damocles threat
Of power-plants' silent leaks
Undoing the bones of a planet.

Clearly the pain of a torn cocoon,
Rip of unclosing
Hearts in manhood's burning noon
Who would follow in their footsteps
At the rising of the moon

On into the blue and risky unknown?
Flourish or perish
As we bend to caress the windblown
Face of mother-earth weeping
Under her broken ozone.

Clearly a grief, an urge to keep
Faith even
With our own fond mistakes. A deep
Gambling unease, a last teetering
Chaos before our leap.

Mesh

Thrill of teetering as lines blur and merge
In media res
Of this our mortal life and still our urge

To withdraw. Yet to refuse to second-guess.
Our step into space
Another free-fall in sweet confusions of process.

Campaigns, cross-border information flows
Keeping pace
Across an atlas, nodes and clusters of NGOs,

Eco-watchers or whistle-blowers who relay
The word in case....
An Ainu website, *médicins sans frontières*,

Circles of Buddhist monks, ghostly chat-rooms
Or face to face,
Amnesty, networks of dwellers in shacks or slums.

Boundless world of hidden loops and re-loops,
A noiseless trace
Of complex feedback and feedforward hoops.

Is something in the making, something new?
Another place
Over and under our boundaries, a reaching through

And linking up both in and beyond regimes,
Fuzzy embrace
Of overlapping maps, our mesh of dreams.

Mending

Something on the go. Something new?
But once our cities' mix and brew –
Alexandria, a nurse of every race.

Once west to east a silken route
Of questing swaps and barter, astute
Venetian Polo crossed to China.

A wrong bearing, any misreading
Unmaps a whole adventure leading
Us astray by slips and blunders.

A fractious Europe, greedy Minotaur
Wandering through thirty years of war,
Side-tracked in cul-de-sacs and alleys.

Then byways of flag and proletariat,
Goose-step of ism and autocrat,
Grimmest hundred years of carnage.

Searching a silken clew to the maze,
We retrace steps to mend our ways.
Something old is harking onwards.

Seepage

Hybrids of old, all our songs and histories ooze:
London reggae, Yiddish tangos, pale-faced blues,

Chaîne de dames danced at *céilís*, *los gauchos judíos*.
Drift and flux of all that's open-ended and porous.

The words we loan that seem to wander and renew;
Proverbs, faiths, motifs, borrowings, seepings through.

Years of rubbing along or just letting things slide,
Ease of decades of trade, our muddling side by side.

Poland's memory of Khazars, Toledo's open mind,
The Koran's *ya ayyuha 'n naasu*, o mankind!

Right but maybe wrong, wrong but maybe right;
In huddles of cities, our days lived in each other's light.

Slow rite of osmosis, aborptions half understood.
Surges and ebbs. Our long sievings of mongrelhood.

Accelerando

Gone the leisure of change. No long, slow
Percolations, trade-offs of loan or swap;
A new upping of pace, daily *accelerando*
Of chance and switches, our choices' flip-flop.
No moss gathering, *Swaraj*, Ourselves Alone.
Together to shuttle a planet's shrunken girth,
Border-crosser, globe-trotter, rolling stone,
All *grenzgänger* now we dwarf our earth.
Constant shadowing in, scumble of old divides,
Topsyturvy world of shifting borderland,
So much of what we thought so certain slides,
To move the earth where's our somewhere to stand?
Glasnost of nanosecond and graven silicon;
Pole to pole our driven sifting cyclotron.

Giant

One-eyed market giant
Driven by haggle and deal
Straddling a whole sphere,

Plateau or atoll,
Desert or jungle basin,
Our earth's four corners.

High-speed, space-shrinking,
One sprawling, planet-girdling
Game of here-there-ness.

Foods or goods or tools,
All chains of commodities,
Our tastes and desires.

Mergers or movements
Of labour, takeover bids,
All the tricks of trade.

Hungry pliant giant,
Bringer of all invention,
Heeder of what works.

Lattice of silk routes.
Worldwide pitch. Grand casino.
Globe of all play all.

Seeing

Once a market's noisy playground,
split difference, spit and luck-penny,
higgle-haggle gossip of a souk,

horses and carts of traders gathered
in the staring light of a *shtetl*'s square
busy unpacking stalls and wares.

But lives eked in favelas and barrios
or bidonvilles as all the while
a giant rumbles across the earth.

Containers, wide-winged jet-craft,
juggernauts swallow all before them.
The strong stronger, the weak weaker.

Rock stars, nomad managers, tycoons;
under four hundred billionaires
belting half our planet's wealth.

Somewhere in slums or refuge camps,
in ramshackle sweat shops or shanty
with fists of stone and clenched teeth

a Gilgamesh grown angry in his youth
seals his heart to fell the cedar
and slay the all-preying ogre.

How now to yoke the avid beast,
a tamed Humbaba broken in
to see what one-eyed giants can't see?

Humbaba

Moody Humbaba, bull and bear,
One-eyed giant of *laissez-faire*,
In open rings no fake control
Up and up the greasy pole,
Make or break, boom or bust,
Winners all or bite the dust.

Life unknown, unseen face,
If a cut's better another place,
Stony eyes on the bottom line
To keep the shareholders benign;
Word from on high and incognito
Take up the silken tent and go.

So on. A circus can't second-guess.
Humbaba whispers success, success.
Full of options doubting Thomas,
Till death or we break our promise;
Where it shifts, where it flows.
Hazy despair of anything goes.

Vague unease. A rogue state,
A lone zealot big with fate,
Some ideologue or malcontent,
A button pressed, anthrax sent,
Half-lulled awareness of a messed
Habitat, our greed-fouled nest?

What unfaced face under the sun
Calls to account what we've undone?
Bargain-driver, giver and taker,
Homo sapiens, meaning maker,
Shaper or shaped, player or plaything,
Are we still masters of our ring?

Loop

Less a ring than another looping back,
Relearning to cross again an older track.

In nooks of harvest fields the forgotten sheaf,
Each seventh year's share-out and debt relief

Bent on offsetting our market's quid pro quo:
A tithe to Levite, sojourner, fatherless, widow

Binding alms beyond whims of goodwill.
Mohammed's urged levy for needy and ill,

For those hearts it's necessary to conciliate;
Ballast and even out, a counter-weight

To those bitter daily shadows of bony hunger.
Someone's birthright is only to die younger?

An overflow shared, our balance re-tipped.
Can we forget the starving years of Egypt?

Update

Given a globe of flash and breaking news
Where swarms of flies on a starving face
Crawl a screen of glass
Between comfort and hunger, refuse

To fade when zapped but leave a creeping trace
Within a psyche's magic lantern,
An after-image of concern,
Given a globe has watched the wasting face

We can no longer say we didn't know.
Gone the slow dispatch our alibi
For hindsight, each plea
Immediate and doubled in its nag and echo

Haunts the ear of every brother's keeper.
Bulletin by bulletin, update by update,
Famine's balance sheet.
Bitter wind-sower, whirlwind reaper

Still so world-foolish and pennywise,
Children's children know we know.
Tomorrow, tomorrow, tomorrow.
Abel's child now starves before our eyes.

Butterfly

Yes now and again to feel so overpowered.
Could anything we ever do matter a whit?
Would-be dreams, seeds that never flowered,
A world just as it is and there you have it!
Yet a fresh belonging, thrill of connectedness,
In the maze and jumble of whatever's new
As if a globe so imperfect in its glorious mess
Catches in spins and webs everything we do.
Beyond fluke or the end of fate's weary tether
Sweet chaos transcends and breaks old spells
As somewhere under the folds of summer sky
A flapped red admiral shifts a planet's weather.
Again everything matters to everything else;
Vision gathers in the span of one butterfly.

Ad Lib

A hazier vision both more and other,
neither state nor superstate, a melding in,
a ravel of pacts and stitched affiliations,

jagged ad lib of patchworks and deals,
sixes and sevens of bonds and ties,
plans caught up in random drift,

bits of schemes as we go along,
spliced, recombinant, spilling over,
shimmies of mimicry, on the spot design,

stop-start modes or toggle switches,
loose weavings, filigrees of consensus
thickening into webs of give and take.

No longer the view from nowhere,
citizens of a planet and still parishioners
we must belong now here, now there,

both a sizing up and a sizing down.
Given a globe of satellite footprints
one half knows how the other lives,

given a globe now to improvise
we hold each other again to account,
players all in our jazz of things.

Shuffle

Our clumsy fellowship of jazz,
Fast and loose of lines revised,
Tunes bedded in our roll and swing.

The jet-setters' razzamatazz,
Messengers of a past now idolised
And each demanding all or nothing.

High-flying soprano saxophone
So heady as it tries to soar
Homelessly above our thick and thin;

A solo trumpets what's our own
Dreaming soundproof rooms before
The blare and clamour, before the din.

O down to earth all players now,
The bob and riff and open-plan.
No opting out. The line evolves,

Even our hearing shaping how
It loops and turns as best it can.
In double listening a clash resolves,

Richer in remembered dissonance.
Argument over argument, by pros
And cons and shuffled compromise,

The counterpoint, the taken chance,
As discord by discord we recompose
And for the music's sake extemporise

Bluesy scales of how we cope.
Neither returning or losing the way,
All vision in rhythms of how it is.

Each-in-otherness, ad hocery of hope
Keeping all our difference in play,
Quarrelsome sessions of beloved noise.

Behind

White noise of all forsaken still insists
Across a high-strung rainbow of snare-drums
On weaving in among the horn and sax

Pitchless sounds astray in cul-de-sacs,
Alleys of broken pasts, consortiums
Of static grief that summon still our shades

To thicken every phrase before it fades
Into indistinctness where soloists
Blur again amid the jazz reminding us

Of each travail and tragedy left behind us
And how out of bones of slaves music wrests
A syncopated note of gaiety that hones

The stories of affliction no one owns,
When brass jams and blows its moody idioms,
Weeping over the stillborn milk of history.

Clusters

Always our histories loop and so renew.
Schools, combos, zones of thought, a few
Tight clutches of friends, bands of dissidence,
Brainstorms, cross-breeding argument, dense
Huddles of players face to face that change
A rhythm's logic, curve our psychic range
To sift and fuse and rearrange progressions
That shape the mood of an age, jam sessions
Over time and the teacher-to-pupil baton:
Socrates, Plato, Aristotle on and on
Or chez Café Guernois Degas, Manet,
Cézanne and Pissarro busy arguing their way
Around their darker masters. Switched modes,
Nests and seedbeds, genealogies of nodes
As Satchmo Armstrong once played with King
Oliver and Jelly Roll. In musics of doing.
Yesterday's not today or now tomorrow's way
Which of course is never simply to say
That though there's no one way there's no
Yardstick and yesterday we sometimes know
Was better or not as good, just as tomorrow
May hoop either way to cobble joy or sorrow
In honky-tonks of being where rhythms swap,
cakewalk, ragtime, jazz, swing or bebop.
Dizzy's and Parker's chopped staccatos stunned
Munroe's Uptown House at 52nd,
A variation become as weighty as a theme,
Fractured melody hovers above a seam
Of chord sequences in a six bar repeat
As accents land now on, now off the beat
In promises of process and substance blended.
Paradox of solo and ensemble in one splendid
Line that knows the moment of ordered freedom
When the brass blows down and yields to drum.
What a man does with his life when it's finally his;
Everywhere is local now exactly where it is.
Beyond a deadlock of perfection in notes that jar
We make each broken other whatever we are.

Polyphony of phrase, each open-hearted probe,
Clusters of goodwill in swap-shops of a globe;
Where music aims the music holds within.
The jazz is as the jazz has never been.

Tremolo

All that has been still an undertone,
Frets of memory half-heard deep
Below a hybrid croon of saxophone

Or when King Oliver's horn's darker
Notes warn a plantation child
He'd die an obscure poolroom marker.

A Bushman taps a hunting bow,
One end humming between the lips,
Drone of sound mesmeric and hollow.

At wedding gigs East Europe's blues
In moods of a harmonic minor scale
Blare a wistful klezmer rumpus.

Fingers strum a blown *mukkuri*
As swung against an Ainu's hips
A song of peace plucks a *tonkori.*

Once Turk or Khan, Rome or Greece,
Empires now where suns never fall,
A dominant bringing a dominant peace.

But one space of chosen nodes,
Mediant world of both/and plays
In flexitime, in different modes?

Given riffs and breaks of our own,
Given a globe of boundless jazz,
Yet still a remembered undertone,

A quivering earthy line of soul
Crying in all diminished chords.
Our globe still trembles on its pole.

Over the Kwai

Trembling, in tears, over and over
I'm very, very sorry. Nagasesan
a tiny man in an elegant straw-hat,
loose kimono-like jacket and trousers
bowed in the heat as the sun clambered
a sky up over the morning Kwai.

Lomax, you will tell us, his once
victim remembered, *Lomax you will*
be killed shortly whatever happens,
a mechanical voice doing its duty
in its choppy menacing segments,
loathsome endless singsong questions.

An officer picked up a big stick.
After Nagasesan had interpreted
every query, a slow deliberate
blow delivered from head height
to his chest, belly and broken arms.
Lomax, you tell us, then it will stop.

The full gush of a nearby hosepipe
turned onto his nostrils and mouth,
a torrent into his lungs and stomach
choking and welling up within;
the voice of Nagasesan heard again
above his head and into his ear.

Fifty years, a long time for me,
for suffering. I never forgot you,
I remember your face, even your eyes...
Nagasesan's long rapids of remembrance
gathering up all unfinished histories
to span the Kwai and ask forgiveness.

Yurusu, to allow, accept, absolve,
a giving away hidden in pardon,
or *maitheamh* our own 'making good'
a victim's fifty lurking years
of lone recall and dreamt revenge.
Lomax, you'll tell us as you let go

the prey of so many broken pasts
walk to greet their once hunter
over a sweated bridge of a memory,
rapprochement of all our ghosts
cross timeless flows of atonement.
We can't forget. We do forgive.

Skeins

Never to forget the towering dreams
Of heaven-hankers before their time,
Brick for stone, for mortar slime

So many offered for madcap schemes.
Over and again some other fable
Of perfection: *Let us make us a name.*

Another skyscraper and still the same.
Fall and fall all spires of Babel
To lovely confusions of our gabble

Scattered abroad on the face of the earth
As slowly we relearn each other's worth,
Difference and sameness incommensurable.

In all our babble birds of a feather –
Aithníonn ciaróg ciaróg eile,
Beetle knows beetle – *Qui se ressemble*

S'assemble – all over flock together,
Skeins of hope, *gleich und gleich...*
Like to like, kind calls fellow –

Rui wa tomo o yobu in Tokyo.
Around our globe a netted Reich,
Of random trust, cross-ties of civility,

Farflung jumbles of non-violent voices
Argue our intertwining choices
To weave one planet's fragile city.

Strategy

Global city of nowhere and everywhere,
Comity of good will,
Delicate growth that thrives
On thriving and yet always so bound

Up with states and their staked out
Limits, a brokerage between
Determined hit-and-runners
Who still think their bombs can pound

An earth to submission and the too naïve
So easily taken for a ride
By every thug and trafficker,
All the more hard-bitten on the rebound.

Our brittle city of Trojan horses,
Hijacked battering rams,
Poison on the market shelf,
Gas canisters in the underground

Or the underminers within the psyche,
Unmasked unmaskers of power's
Bleak and stalking beast,
Suspicious minds that never unwound.

Give us a policy? At least a strategy?
The slow hatchings of peace,
Our stumbled unfinishedness
Dealing with everything just as it's found,

A trust in openness, the barer daring
Of players out on a limb;
No iron curtain here,
Fragile theatre of worlds in the round.

Bridges

Around our Babel-fallen world
embedded in grammars of landscape,
jumble and palaver of simultaneity

as though on one Rabelaisian earth
in myriad difference grains of sameness,
Seeds of everything in everything else,

the way white light contains all waves
and a sound wakes its every partial
or from one cell any limb unfolds.

Still our heartlands and inner sources',
quiet meanderings of each particular.
Yet given a globe of such opulence

will one-tongued markets ever hear
how watchwords in so many lores
admonish against too muddied waters?

Over our years a Dante is warning:
l'aqua cheta rovina i ponti –
Stagnant water demolishes bridges.

Deepest river, least its noise
in worlds kept by core keepers
where stiller waters still run deep.

Session

Deep, deep
The legends and contours of every line,
Tune womb
Of our stories of who begat whom,
And as phrases part or combine.

So fine
A line between what's open and shut.
Proud horns
Above a shivering reed that mourns
What never made the cut.

Power's glut
Of power knows always what's true.
Somewhere
Against the grain, again the flair
Among a jazz's daring few

Some new
Delight in playing face to face
Grace notes
For a line that steadies as it floats,
Without a theory or a base,

Shared space
Holding what we hold and not to fear
Those bars
Where our history clashes or jars
And in lines unsymmetrical to the ear

Still hear
Deep reasonings of a different lore.
No map
Of any middle ground or overlap
Yet listening as never before –

No more –
Just hunched jazzmen so engrossed
In each
Other's chance outleap and reach
Of friendship at its utmost.

No host
And no one owns the chorus or break.
Guests all
At Madam Jazz's beck and call.
For nothing but the music's sake.

Only End

Music of a given globe,
Off-chance jazz forever bringing
More being into being
Out of history's tangled knots and loops
Spirituals and flophouse bands
In hymns and charismatic whoops,
In night-clubs' vibe and strobe,
Nothing buts now *everything ands.*

Our heads are ancient Greeks
Who think just because they think
A body's out of sync
With thought but maybe we relearn the way
Our mind can pulse to intransigent
Musics of once broken to play
Beyond perfect techniques
The livelong midrash of a moment.

Given a globe of profusion,
We players are no legislators
More like mediators,
Who extemporising seem to up the ante
To find the nit and grit that has
A universal image for a Dante,
An aim without conclusion
To play mein host to Madam Jazz

Playing without end.
Growling, wailing, singing Madam
In anguish and joys we jam
As Davis's almost vibratoless horn
Wraps around *Embraceable You*
Somehow original and still reborn
Swooping back to mend,
Resolving just to clash again.

All time to understand
Infinite blues of what ifs,
Breaks and tragic riffs
As traditions wander into other spaces
Zigzagging and boundary crossing
In clustered face-to-faces
Commonplace and grand,
Sweet nuisances of our being

On song and off-beam,
Hanging loose, hanging tough,
Offbeat, off the cuff,
Made, broken and remade in love,
Lived-in boneshaking pizzazz
Of interwoven polyphony above
An understated theme.
The only end of jazz is jazz.

Micheal O'Siadhail was born in 1947. He was educated at Clongowes Wood College, Trinity College Dublin, and the University of Oslo. A full-time writer, he has published eleven collections of poetry. He was awarded an Irish American Cultural Institute prize for poetry in 1982, and the Marten Toonder Prize for Literature in 1998. His poem suites, *The Naked Flame*, *Summerfest*, *Crosslight* and *Dublin Spring* were commissioned and set to music for performance and broadcasting.

His latest collections are *Our Double Time* (1998), *The Gossamer Wall: poems in witness to the Holocaust* (2002), *Love Life* (2005) and *Globe* (2007), all published by Bloodaxe. *Hail! Madam Jazz: New and Selected Poems* (Bloodaxe Books, 1992) included selections from five of his early collections, *The Leap Year* (1978), *Rungs of Time* (1980), *Belonging* (1982), *Springnight* (1983) and *The Image Wheel* (1985), as well as the whole of *The Chosen Garden* (1990) and a new collection, *The Middle Voice* (1992). A new selection of his earlier poetry, *Poems 1975-1995*, drawing on both *Hail! Madam Jazz* and his later collection *A Fragile City* (Bloodaxe Books, 1995), was published by Bloodaxe in 1999.

He has given poetry readings and broadcast extensively in Ireland, Britain, Europe, North America and Japan. In 1985 he was invited to give the Vernam Hull Lecture at Harvard and the Trumbull Lecture at Yale University. He represented Ireland at the Poetry Society's European Poetry Festival in London in 1981. He was writer-in-residence at the Yeats Summer School in 1991 and read at the Frankfurt Bookfair in 1997.

He has been a lecturer at Trinity College Dublin and a professor at the Dublin Institute for Advanced Studies. Among his many academic works are *Learning Irish* (Yale University Press, 1988) and *Modern Irish* (Cambridge University Press, 1989). He was a member of the Arts Council of the Republic of Ireland (1988-93) and of the Advisory Committee on Cultural Relations (1989-97), a founder member of Aosdána (Academy of distinguished Irish artists) and a former editor of *Poetry Ireland Review*. He is the founding chairman of ILE (Ireland Literature Exchange), and was a judge for *The Irish Times* ESB 1998 Theatre Awards and the 1998 *Sunday Tribune*/Hennessy Cognac Literary Awards.

Micheal O'Siadhail's website: www.osiadhail.com